JE DOIS COLORIER, VOUS DEVEZ FOUTRE LE CAMP!

UN LIVRE DE COLORIAGE POUR ADULTES REMPLI DE MAGNIFIQUES GROS MOTS

MONIQUE SABINE

PARDON MY FRENCH
PRESS

All rights reserved. No part of this book may be reproduced or used in any way or form or by any means whether electronic or mechanical, this means that you cannot record or photocopy material ideas or tips that are provided in this book.

ABOUT THE FRENCH WORDS AND PHRASES IN THIS COLORING BOOK

Hi, Monique here! Okay, the chart on the next page lists all of the French words and phrases used in the designs in this book, what they mean, and how to pronounce them. (Feel free to tear the page out and carry it with you or post it at your workspace for easy reference.)

The best way to learn how to say these, however, is to hear them spoken aloud. The easiest way to do that (other than asking a French-speaking friend or relative) is to just follow these steps:

1. Head on over to the Web here: https://www.howtopronounce.com/french/index.php. (You might want to bookmark this page, you'll probably want to come back here a lot. By the way, should this page be unavailable, just search for another "French pronunciation" page — there's lots of them.)

2. Copy a word from the chart and paste it into the box.

3. Click the **Pronounce** button.

4. A new page displays. On this page, click on the word you just entered (shown in purple). Another new page displays.

5. On this page, click the purple speaker icon next to your word (which is now in green, at the top of the page). You'll hear a native speaker say the word for you.

6. Keep clicking! Listen and repeat again and again until you have it down cold. You are now ready to drop that French bomb when needed (which will be soon!) Tres bien!

Have fun learning French, one swear word at a time!

Love ♡,
Monique xoxo

PLEASE STAY IN TOUCH!

Here's how you can contact me:
* www.pardonmyfrenchpress.com/monique
* https://www.facebook.com/PardonMyFrenchPress
* monique.sabine@pardonmyfrenchpress.com

AND, IF YOU'D BE SO KIND, PLEASE LEAVE A REVIEW!

If you love my first French swear words coloring book, let me know. Leaving a review is just like telling your friends about this book. If you feel like sharing (and maybe showing off a bit!), snap a pic of one of your finished pages and post it along with your review, too. Post it to my Facebook page, as well, to share it and get Likes and praises, and maybe even some fans and new friends!

Thank you ♡ ♡!

Drawing	French Word or Phrase	English Meaning	Pronunciation
1	chier!	shit! (or, crap!)	"shay" or "shee-yair"
2	bite	cock	"beet"
3	fils de salope	son of a bitch	"feez day sah-lope"
4	abruti	asshole!	"ah-britty"
5	putain t'es moche	you're fuckin' UGLY! / you're an ugly whore!	"pe-tahn tay mohsh"
6	gross cul	big butt	"gross coo"
7	vous etes stupide	you're stupid	"vooz-atay stupeed-ah"
8	tu m`emmerdes	you're bullshittin' me	"too em ah-murdah"
9	connard	asshole!	"coo-nah"
10	zut	heck! or darn!	"yoot"
11	conneries	bullshit	"con-ree"
12	va te faire foutre	go fuck yourself	"vah too fair foot-ruh"
13	meurs, pute	die, bitch!	"mahr-pyoot"
14	putain	whore!	"pee-tahn"
15	branleur	a jerk-off or 'wanker'	"brawn-lerr"
16	me sucer la bite	suck my dick	"moo sol-see lah beet"
17	salaud	bastard	"sal-loo"
18	tais-toi!	shut up!	"tay-twaw"
19	face de cul	ass face	"fahs do cool"
20	brûle en enfer	burn in hell	"breel-lon on fair"
21	truie	pig	"twee"
22	merde	shit! (or, crap!)	"mare-duh"
23	fais chier	damn it!	"fesh-shay"
24	vous vissez	screw you!	"voo-vee-see"
25	salope	slut!	"sah-lope"
26	baise	fuck[1]	"bay-zuh"
27	petite pute	little bitch / little whore	"pa-teet pyoot"
28	ça craint	this sucks	"see-ya crun"

Drawing	French Word or Phrase	English Meaning	Pronunciation
29	fous le camp	fuck off!	"foo-loo camp"
30	fils de pute[2]	son of a whore	"feez day pyoot"
31	ferme ta putain de gueule connard	shut the fuck up, asshole	"firm nah pea-tahn dur gehl coo-nah"
32	tu es con	you're dumb	"too ay cohn"
33	manges la merde	eat shit	"manj lay mare-duh"
34	débile	moron	"duh-veal-uh"
35	garce	slut	"garse"
36	sac-merde	shit bag	"sock mare-duh"
37	mon dieu	my God!	"mahn djoo"
38	ta mere la pute	your mother is a whore	"tah mair lah pyoot"
39	ta gueule	shut up! / shut your trap!	"tah goal-lah"
40	t'es débile	you're an idiot	"tee duh-veal-uh"
BONUS	va te faire foutre, trouduc	Fuck you, asshole!	"vah too fair foot-ruh tro-dic"

[1] Can also mean, funny enough, "kiss."
[2] Can also be used as a substitute for "motherfucker."